Contents

The Basics of Finding a Work-At-Home Job

Wouldn't it be nice to roll out of bed, slip on a robe and slippers and shuffle down the hall to your home office to work? Today over 137 million people world-wide do just that at least part time as more as more companies take advantage of the cost savings that telecommuting programs offer. One of the best places to find these companies is online. But you must be careful when searching for work-at-home jobs. While opportunities for work-at-home employment continue to grow, so does the risk of getting scammed.

What you need to know!

Before embarking on your work-at-home job search, there are few key rules you need to understand.

1) You can't sign up for a work-at-home job. Telecommuting work is found in the same way that traditional work is found. You need skills, experience and a professional resume.

2) You can't pay to get hired. Any company that says you can work for it by sending money is not offering a job. It's okay to invest in a good work-at-home job database or hiring a professional resume writer, but never pay to get hired. Let me add that a legitimate company will never need to use your personal bank account to do business either.

3) To increase the odds of getting a work-at-home job, be open to many job types. Instead of thinking, "I want to sit home and type," consider all the skills you have that can be used at home. Are you a good researcher? Do you have good phone skills? Are you highly organized? Are you creative? Can you write persuasively? Make a list of all your skills, experiences, talents and hobbies and search for jobs that need those attributes.

4) Look for work where jobs are posted. Most people get in trouble because they look for the wrong types of jobs in the wrong places. Use job search sites not search engines to find work-at-home jobs. Check out reputable work-at-home resources to learn about working at home and also to get job leads.

5) Be professional. I can't believe some of the email I receive from people who tell me they can type and yet their email is full of typos and grammatical errors. Or they say they want to work at home, but provide no information on what they are qualified to do. You have one chance to convince a potential employer that you can do the job. The employer doesn't care about your childcare hassles or illness. She only cares about finding the best person to do the job. All your interactions should focus on what you can do for the employer.

6) Learn a skill that is in high demand. There are certain job types that have many job openings right now such as copywriting, customer service, web and graphic design, medical transcription, writers and more. If you can't do any of these jobs, why not learn? Most can be either self-taught or learned through an online or correspondence course.

Today, the opportunities to work from home are endless and continue to grow. But to get hired, it's important to understand what work-at-home jobs are, why companies offer them, and how you can position yourself to get hired. By understanding the six telecommuting rules outlined here, you will find legitimate jobs faster and improve your chances of getting hired.

Three Steps to Getting a Work-At-Home Job

Each week I find hundreds of work-at-home job announcements from companies looking for qualified employees to hire. Despite the abundance of work-at-home jobs, millions of people who want a work-at-home job continue to fall victim to scams and deceptive schemes. If you have been struggling to work at home, here are the three steps you must follow to be successful.

Step One: What can you do?

You wouldn't use a search engine and sign up for the first thing that sounded good in a traditional job search; yet, so many people take this approach to finding a work-at-home job. One of the most important concepts you need to understand is that ***work-at-home job searches are just like traditional job searches***. Employers are looking for people with skills and experience to fill specific jobs. You won't simply sign up for a work-at-home job. Instead you'll need a professional resume or application that sets you apart from the competition. All this starts by listing your skills and experiences. Don't limit this list just to job skills. Also include volunteer experience, hobbies, and interests. Take note of the duties and activities your "jobs" involved and the things you've learned from your experiences.

Step Two: Look for jobs

Most people get in trouble in their work-at-home job search because they look for the wrong jobs in the wrong places. In Step One you learned that work-at-home jobs are no different from traditional jobs and as a result you've made a list of all your experiences. In Step Two you need to begin to search where employers post jobs. You can find work-at-home job announcements on job sites such as Monster.com and Careerbuilder.com by using "work at home" (in quotes) or "telecommute" (quotes not needed) as your keyword. You still need to watch out for deceptive job ads on general job search sites. The best way to avoid them is to remember two rules: 1) never pay money to get hired and 2) never give or use your personal bank to help a company do business.

If you're serious about finding a work-at-home job, consider using a work-at-home job database. These services are not free (you're not paying to get hired, you're paying for the service of having someone else screen work-at-home jobs and allowing you to access their database), but they make finding jobs fast and easy. You'll find a list of general and telecommuting job search website at the end of this book.

Step Three: Apply, Apply, Apply

A successful job search requires creating a stellar resume or application. Remember, you're competing against hundreds, maybe even thousands of other applicants. Your resume or application needs to set you apart from all of them. You do that by tailoring your resume to the specific skills and experiences the employer is looking for. If the ad is for a transcriptionist to help a public speaker, share how fast you type, whether or not you have transcribed for other speakers or in the topic area the speaker specializes in. Indicate specific equipment or software you have experience with. Fit the resume to the job and you'll be showing the employer you're the exact person he's looking for.

Also, do as the application says, no more, no less. A common complaint with employers is that the applicants don't follow the directions. Don't try to be cute or creative. Use strong, active verbs to outline your skills instead of crazy font or gimmicks.

Finally be ready to apply to many jobs over time. Work-at-home employers are notorious for not getting back to applicants about their submissions, so you need to keep applying, following-up, finding more jobs and applying some more. Successful home-based employees find their jobs by never giving up the search.

With hundreds of employers looking for qualified home-based workers, the would-be telecommuter has many opportunities to find a job. However, like traditional jobs, work-at-home jobs are earned by showcasing skills and experiences.

Avoid a Work-At-Home Job Scam

Each year, millions of people fall victim to work-at-home job scams. This happens despite all the great information in books and online on how to identify legitimate work-at-home programs and avoid scams.

One reason that people still get caught up in scams is because they look for the wrong kind of work in the wrong place. As a result, they are exposed to more scams and don't ever find the real jobs.

Scams to Avoid

- Typing (although you may find a job in transcription)
- Envelope stuffing
- Assembly work
- Data entry (there are a few -- very few-- legitimate data entry jobs)
- Email processing
- Rebate processing
- Transaction processing (or anything that asks you to use your personal bank account or credit card to do business)
- Refund tracer
- Ad placer
- Web surfer
- Survey taker (You can win prizes and sometimes earn a little cash, but it's not a job.)
- Sign-up-do-nothing schemes. This may seem obvious, but I find work-at-home offers all the time that suggest you can make millions just by signing up.
- Any "job" that requires a fee to get started.

Email Job Scams

There are scammers who send emails that suggest they are in response to your job submission. In most cases you can weed them out because they don't use your name, don't provide a company name and don't indicate the job title for which you applied. But scammers are clever and this could change. I recommend that you keep a list of all the jobs you apply to including the name of the company and title of the job so you can check email responses against your list. Legitimate responses will have the name of the company, the job title to which you applied to and nearly always will be addressed specifically to you.

Cyber-Resumes for Work-At-Home Jobs

In the cyber-world as in the real world, your resume and cover letter are the first chance you have to make an impression on a potential employer. A well- written resume shows that you are professional and will help you proceed to the next step in the job hiring process. A resume that falls short in terms of providing relevant information or a sense of professionalism will be discarded. Do not let your work-at-home resume end up in the reject pile.Before sending your resume and cover letter to a potential employer, check to make sure you follow the guidelines below:

Do:

- Follow the job announcement's instruction for applying to the job.
- Limit your resume to one page.
- Use 12-pt font size.
- Avoid fancy style fonts and formats. Not all computers can accurately decipher special fonts and formatting (i.e. bold, italics).
- Spell out all abbreviations; even those that should be obvious.
- Include your full name, address, telephone number and e-mail in all documents.
- Outline relevant work experience using your most recent occupation first.
- If you are recent graduate, consider listing your education before your work experience.
- List other relevant experience such as volunteer work, certifications, course work, etc.
- If possible, address your cover or introductory letter to a specific person. You can get this from the job announcement or the company's web site.
- Your letter of introduction should include the position to which you are applying and where you saw the position advertised.
- Highlight your skills and experience that are specific to the job in the body of your letter.
- Proofread, proofread, and proofread your resume and letter of introduction (cover letter). It doesn't matter how qualified you are for the job if your resume has typos and grammatical errors.

Don't:

- List skills or experience that are unrelated to the position offered in your resume or cover letter.
- Exaggerate or falsify anything.
- Give personal information such as marital status, age, etc.
- Have any grammatical or typographical errors.
- Use a personal or buddy-like tone in your cover letter.
- Send bulk, generic resumes and cover letters.
- Sound desperate. Companies want the best person for the job. Your financial situation will not sway a decision one way or another.
- Be over enthusiastic. 'Salesmen' type hype does not impress employers.
- Refer to yourself in the third person in your cover letter. Instead, use "I", and "me", etc.
- Send your resume as an attachment unless you are told specifically to do so. Most companies delete e-mail with attachments for security purposes.

Sources for Work-At-Home Jobs

In this section, you'll find hundreds of places you can use to find work-at-home jobs. Some of these sources charge a fee to access their database. Remember, these sources aren't selling you a job. They are providing you with a service of delivering screened work-at-home jobs. I always recommend that you start with the free options.

Sites that List Telecommuting Jobs

These sites are free and fee-based resources for finding work at home jobs. Please review the scam information as sometimes scams or non-job opportunities can get listed on these sites.

2Work-At-Home.com
FlexJobs
HomeJobStop $
Rat Race Rebellion
SOHO Jobs – Free and ($)
Telecommuting Job Opportunities $
VirtualAssistance.com $
WAHM
Work-At-Home Success

General Freelance Work

Elance ($)
Guru
HomeworkersNet
Odesk
Workaholics4Hire

Freelance Job Resources—Computer and IT Work

Computer Jobs
Contract Job Hunter
Dice
JustTechJobs
Planet Recruit Search using "Freelance."
Project Spring ($)
VWorker

Freelance Writing Work
Absolute Writers
Avalanche of Jobs
Freelance Writing
Freelance Writing Gigs
MediaBisto
ProBlogger
WritersWeekly.com

General Job Search Web sites
These sites offer general job announcements. Once you access the Web site, use keywords such as "telecommute" and "work at home" to search the databases.

United States Job Search web sites
6 Figure Jobs
AdQuest3-D
CareerBuilder Network
Career Journal from the Wall Street Journal
Employment911
Flipdog
Job.com
Jobs.com
Job Central
JobHunt
KellyCareerNetwork
Monster.com
Net-Temps
True Careers
WorkTree.com $
Yahoo HotJobs

Regional Northeast Job Search Web sites
Boston Works
Boston Job Bank
Find It Online
New Jersey Online
Philadelphia Job Net

Companies that Accept Applications for Contract Workers

These companies frequently accept applications for home-based workers. Where possible I have provided links right to the job information page; however, some pages require that you click on a link from the home page. For those listings you'll see directions on what to click.

Websites are updated and changed frequently and you may find that some links to the career pages don't work. If that is the case, access the main site (eliminate the page address and instead go to the main domain, ie: if its abc.com/careers.html that isn't working, go to abc.com and see if there is a link to careers from there). You can contact me here to let me know about links that aren't working.

Some companies hire both home-based and onsite staff, so you'll need to read the job information carefully to identify the telecommuting opportunities.

I cannot guarantee that these companies are hiring right now or that they provide steady, ongoing work. These companies indicate on their websites that they accept applications for home-based workers. With that said, you'll need to meet the requirements the companies outline for being considered for work.

Administrative Support/Virtual Assistants/Data Entry/General Transcription/Captioning
Absolute Docs
AccuTran Global
Alderson Reporting
Alice Darling Secretarial Services, Inc
American High Tech Transcription
Axion Data
Cambridge Transcription
Capital Typing
Caption Colorado
Continental Promotion Group
CyberDictate
Dion Data Solutions
Diversified Reporting
DriverGuide.com (database entry of device drivers)
Edge Virtual Assistance

eScriptionists
eTranscription Solutions
ExecuScribe
Expedict
Express Document Service, Inc
Fantastic Transcripts
Mass Transcription
Morningside Partners
Mountain West Processing
Mulberry Studio
Net Transcripts
Office Team
Palm Coast Data (Palm Coast Florida Residents)
Production Transcripts
Purple Shark
SpeakWrite
TASK Transcription
Team Double Click
Tigerfish (transcription)
Transcription 2000
Transcription Studio
TruTranscripts
Ubiqus Reporting
Viable Technologies (transcription)
Virtual Assistants
VITAC Real Time Captioning
Wordz Xpressed
Working Solutions

Accounting/Bookkeeping/Financial/Real Estate
Accountants International
American Title Inc
Balance Your Books
Bateman & Co. Inc, P.C. (click on employment)
Bookminders (need to live in S. PA)
Click Accounts
ClickNWork

Dotun and Casserly
Jelly Bean Services (mortgage loan processors)
Nationwide Loan Processors
OSI Business Services
Tad Accounting
Total Business Care
VT Audit
Warrener Stewart

Communities Guides / Experts / Consultants
About.com
Bella Online
Cha Cha Guide
Clarity Consultants
Dissertation Advisors
Guideline
Just Answer
Live Person
National Seminars Training

Customer Service/Teleservices
1-800Contacts
1-800Flowers
27/7 In Touch (Canada)
AAA Renewals
Accolade Support
AccuConference
ACD Direct
Advanis
Affina
Alpine Access
American Airlines
Ansafone Communications
APAC Customer Service
Arise
ARO Business Process Outsourcing
Auralog
Blue Zebra

Call Center International
Call Center Options
Channel Blend
Cloud 10 Corporation
Connect2Agent
Convergys
Customer Loyalty Concepts
Customer Service Review
DeRosa
eCallogy
Expert Business Development
Extended Presence
GE Call Centers
Grindstone
Hire Point
Hilton Reservations
HSN
ICT Group / Sykes
InfoCision
JLodge
JetBlue
LiveOps
Lunar Pages
Medco
MicahTek, Inc
N.E.W.
Next Level Solutions
O'Currance Teleservices
OnPoint Advocacy
Prince Market Research
Progressive Business Publications
Public Opinion Research
SCI Live
Service 800
Sutherland At Home
TeLCare
The Call Center Inc

Time Communications
U-Haul
Ver-A-Fast
VIP Desk
Voice Log
West At Home
Westat
Working Solutions
XAct Services

Disabled Employees
Barrier Free Choices
Lift, Inc
NTI Central

Human Resources/Recruiting
Career Search Consultants
Dierdra Moire Corporation
EEG Recruiting
Enid, Chesterfield and Co.
Healthcare Recruiters International
HR Advice
IRES, Inc
Pioneer Staffing

Law/Legal Transcription/Mock Juror Jobs
Cambridge Transcription
Counsel On Call
CyberDictate
eJury (mock juror)
eTypist
Hire Counsel
Jelly Bean Services
Jury Test (mock jurors)
Mass Transcription
MicroMash Bar Review (click on Apply to be a Mentor)
Online Verdict (mock jurors)
Neal R. Gross

Real Solutions LCC (real estate closings)
SPI
TASK Transcription
Trial Juries (mock jurors)
Trial Practices (mock jurors)
TypeWrite (legal transcription)

Medical / Nursing (not including medical transcription or coding)
Doctors On Demand
Fonemed
Imaging On Call
Medzilla (job search)
United Health Group
Virtual Radiologic

Medical Transcription and Coding
Accurate Typing Services
AccuScribe
AccuTran Global
Advanced Transcription
American Transcription Solutions
Amphion Medical
Applied Medical Services
Arrendale Associates, Inc
Ascend Health Care
Aviacode
CCS Transcription
Code Busters (click on Join Us)
Complete Coding Solutions
DSG Medical Transcription Solutions
EFD Transcription Service
Expedite (British Columbia, Canada)
ExecuScribe
Express Document Services, Inc
Focus Infomatics
LexiCode
Mag Mutual
MD-IT

MediGrafix
MedQuist
MXSecure
NJPR
Oracle Transcription
Outsourcing Solutions, Inc
Perfect Transcription
Personal Touch Coding Solutions
Phoenix Medcom
Precyse Solutions (type "work at home" in the search box)
Presynct Technologies, Inc
Professional Medical Services, Inc
ScribeCare (scroll down to Career)
Skilled Transcription Services
SpectraMedi
Spheris
SPI
StatIQ Solutions
StenoMed, Inc
SuperScript Medical Transcription
The Coding Network
Thomas Transcription
Torres-Lich & Assoc. Inc
Transcend
TransHealth
Trans Tech Medical Solutions
TRX
Ubiquis (click on Working for Ubiquis)
United Medical Transcription

Miscellaneous Jobs (jobs that don't fit into another category)
Aria (card writing) St. Cloud, MN
Cherry Lane Music Co. (guitar transcribers, piano arrangers, educational
writers)
EBI (background screening)
Face the World (student exchange rep)
Hausernet (mail decoy)

Opuzz Voice (voice talent)
RecruitZone (athletic recruiting)
Write On (hand writing) Fredrick,MD

Notary Jobs
AES Title
American Signing Connection, LLC
American Title Inc
CDS Signing
Signing Source Inc
Vital Signing Inc

PR/Marketing
Partner Centric (Internet marketing)

Research Jobs
AB Check Court Researcher
Accurate Background (court researchers)
Background Profiles (court researchers)
Clicknwork
Harvey E. Morse, P.A.
Information Technologies (court abstractors/data collectors)
JellyBean Services
National Background Screening (court researchers)
Sunlark Resarch (court researchers)
United Data Network (court researchers)
Yahoo

Sales/Appointment Setting/Telemarketing/Fundraising
Arise
Blue Zebra Appointment Setting
Cruise.com
Extended Presence
Grindstone
Great American Opportunities (fundraising sales)
TelereachJobs
Telexpertise

Translation, Interpreter, and Language Services

ABC Translation Services
Accurapid Translation
African Translation
Berlitz
Bilingva
Bridge Linguatec
Butler Hill Group
Creative English Solutions (Canada)
Dialog One
Global Link Translation
Japan Pacific Publications
Language Translation
Language Line Services
Languages Unlimited
Linguistic Systems Inc
Lion Bridge
Multilingual Vacancies
Network Omni
Open World Multilingual Services
Pacific Interpreters
SDL
Set Systems
Telelanguage
The Linguist List
Translators Café
Ubiqus Reporting
UC Translations
We-Translate
Win Translation

Travel/Consierge
Consierge At Large (click on careers)
VIP Desk (conierge)

Tutoring/ Teaching/ Education/ Homework Help
Admissions Consultants
Aim For A Tutoring
American Intercontinental University

Berlitz Language Instructors sp
Bilingual America (Instructors)
BrainMass
Brainfuse
Course Bridge
Creating Careers (UK)
Creative English Solutions (Canada)
Chronicle
Connections Academy
CyberEdit, Inc
Dissertation Advisors
ECOT (Substitute Teachers)
EduWizards
Electronic Classroom of Tomorrow
ETS (click on Careers)
Expert Tutors
Explore eLearning
Free World U (flash card writers)
Global Scholar
Growing Stars
Homework Help
Homework Tutoring
Idapted
Kidspan
Learners Paradise
Limu
McTutor
NimbleMind
Online Learning
Pearson Educational Assessment (at home scorers)
Smart Thinking
Student Questions
Topics Education
Tutor.com
Universal Class
University of California, Berkeley Online Extension
Virtual University

Western Governors University
WyzAnt

Writing / Artists
Some listings in this section are job boards for writers. I have included them
because they are specific resources for writers that have current jobs.
Academic Work (editors/translators)
Appingo
Brandon Hall
Beauty Care
Clicknwork
ComputerJobs.com (technical writing)
CyberEdit
Demand Studios (writers and editors for a variety of topics)
Diversified Reporting
EditFast
FabJob.com
Freelance Writing
FreeP
Fuze
Investigative Reporters and Editors
Journalism Jobs
Just Tech Writer Jobs
McMurry Copy Editor Jobs
Metaphor Studio
Poe War
Proofread Now
Recycled Paper Greetings
Roman and Littlefield Publishing
Self Help Guides
Simply English Proofreading
Sun Oasis
UC Berkeley Journalism Jobs
Victory Productions
Weblogs
WordFirm
Writer Find

The Next Step

Having information and resources is only helpful if you use it. If you're serious about getting a work-at-home job, now is the time to take action. If you haven't made your list of skills, experiences, interests and hobbies, do it now. Then you need to...

1. Identify jobs that need your skills, experience etc.

2. Create a resume template that you can tweak for each job you apply for.

3. Review the list of companies that frequently hire to see if any fit your job skills.

4. Visit company website to learn what is required to get hired.

5. Tailor your resume or application to fit the needs of the employer.

6. Submit your resume.

7. Keep track of all your submissions.

If you've exhausted the list of companies or don't find a company that needs your skills, start search for work.

1. Use the list of job announcement resource to do your search.

2. Review the scam information to help you weed out the jobs from the biz ops and scams.

3. Read the job announcement carefully so you can tailor your resume to fit the needs of the job.

4. Submit your resume.

5. Track all your submissions.

Reminder about Job Email Scams:

I mentioned this earlier, but I want to remind you that there are scammers who send emails suggesting they are in response to your job submission. In most cases you can weed them out because they don't use your name, don't provide a company name and don't indicate the job title for which you applied. But scammers are clever and this could change. That is why you